Coronal Variation in the Pronunciation of Chinese Characters in Mandarin

by

Stephen M Kraemer

In my previous volume entitled, <u>Let's Learn Mandarin Phonics</u> (2017), examples of seven types of phonetic compound characters, based on the syllable structure of Modern Standard Mandarin were given:

- Totally Perfect
- Segment Perfect
- Final Perfect
- Final-Tone Perfect
- Initial Perfect
- Initial-Tone Perfect
- Tone Perfect.

In addition to looking at the pronunciation of phonetic compound characters and their corresponding phonetic element characters, one can look at the pronunciation of individual characters in Mandarin. A number of characters in modern Mandarin have more than one pronunciation, and by comparing these alternate pronunciations of a Mandarin character, one can see several regular patterns of occurrence in these variations. The following are some of the more common patterns of variation in individual character pronunciation in Mandarin:

(1) Segment Perfect Variation

In this pattern, the various pronunciations of an individual character retain the same segment pronunciation, and vary only in their tone. An example is the character 号 , which is pronounced either hào or háo.

(2) Initial Perfect Variation

In this pattern, an individual character has more than one pronunciation, but each character pronunciation begins with the same initial consonant. An example is the character 百 , which is pronounced either bǎi or bó .

(3) Homorganic Initial Variation

In this pattern, the alternate pronunciations of an individual character exhibit a similar initial consonant, namely an initial consonant with the same place of articulation in modern Mandarin. An example is the character 伽 , which is pronounced either qié or jiā. Both pronunciations begin with the same place of articulation, namely a palatal initial, either "q" [tɕʰ] or "j" [tɕ].

In the current volume, individual characters that exhibit Coronal Initial Variation in their pronunciation will be listed. These are characters that share a coronal feature in their initial consonant pronunciation (See Duanmu 2007). This includes characters that exhibit any two of the following categories of initial consonant pronunciation:

an alveolar initial
(d t n l) [t tʰ n l], a dental initial
(z c s) [ts tsʰ s], an alveopalatal
(retroflex) initial (zh ch sh r) [tʂ
tʂʰ ʂ ʐ], or a palatal initial (j q x)
[tɕ tɕʰ ɕ] consonant (See
Kratochvil 1968).

Characters in this study are
also organized according to the
pattern of finals and/or tones
exhibited by the various
pronunciations of an
individual character as
follows:

Tone Perfect

Similar Vowel

Tone Perfect-Similar Vowel

Rime Perfect

Rime-Tone Perfect

Ending Perfect

Ending Perfect-Similar Vowel

Ending-Tone Perfect

Ending-Tone- Perfect-Similar Vowel

Final Perfect

Final-Tone Perfect

Character pronunciations are given using the pinyin alphabet and are taken from Xin Hua Zidian (1971). In cases where individual characters exhibit certain similar vowel or ending patterns, the character pronunciations may be given in both pinyin and IPA. This is done for characters with alternate pronunciations that share a common vowel [u], where the vowel [u] is spelled with either "u" or "o" in pinyin.

Coronal Pronunciation Variation

伧 cāng, chen

侧 cè, zhāi

差 chà, cī

腊 là, xī

喏 rě, nuò

色 sè, shǎi

石 shí, dàn

挲 suō, sha

歙 xī, shè

侧 zhāi, zè

Tone Perfect

差 chā, cī

车 chē, jū

俶 chù, tì

咀 jǔ, zuǐ

率 shuài, lǜ

莎 suō, shā

嘘 xū, shī

畜 xù, chù

择 zé, zhái

柞 zuò, zhà

Similar Vowel

缴 jiǎo[tɕiǎu],
zhuó[tʂuó]

尿 niào[niàu],
suī[suēi]

祇 qí, zhǐ

食 shí, sì

俟 sì, qí

宿 sù, xiǔ

Tone Perfect-Similar Vowel

拆 chāi, cā

差 chāi, cī

翟 dí, zhái

蹢 dí, zhí

似 sì, shì

宿 sù, xiù

吱 zhī, zī

Rime Perfect

剿 jiǎo, chāo

鞘 qiào, shāo

粘 zhān, nián

奘 zhuǎng, zàng

Rime-Tone Perfect

仇 chóu, qiú

臭 chòu, xiù

缲 qiāo, sāo

厦 shà, xià

苕 tiáo, sháo

Ending Perfect

帱 chóu[tʂʰóu], dào[tàu]

酖 dān, zhèn

糁 shēn, sǎn

溱 zhēn, qín

Ending Perfect-Similar Vowel

泷 lóng [lúŋ],
shuāng[ʂuāŋ]

僮 zhuàng[tʂuàŋ],
tóng[tʰúŋ]

Ending-Tone Perfect

参 cān, shēn

铛 dāng, chēng

丁 dīng, zhēng

莘 shēn, xīn

省 shěng, xǐng

覃 tán, qín

Ending-Tone Perfect-Similar Vowel

靓 jìng, liàng

衰 shuāi, cuī

Final Perfect

孱 chán, càn

澄 chéng, dèng

单 dān, chán

单 dān, shàn

掸 dǎn, shàn

蹲 dūn, cún

倘 tǎng, cháng

屯 tún, zhūn

裼 xī, tì

咋 zǎ, zhā

扎 zhá, zā

咋 zhà, zǎ

Final-Tone Perfect

嚓 cā, chā

耑 duān, zhuān

堆 duī, zuī

蜡 là, zhà

挲 sa, sha

参 shēn, cēn

怂 sōng, zhōng

扎 zhā, zā

赚 zhuàn, zuàn

References

Cheng, C.C. (1973). *A synchronic phonology of Mandarin Chinese*. The Hague: Mouton.

Duanmu, San. (2007). *The phonology of standard Chinese.* Second Edition. New York: Oxford University Press.

Handian [<汉典>, '字典']. Online Chinese dictionary. (2004 – 2015). http://www.zdic.net

Kraemer, Stephen M. (1980). *Potentially pedalgogically useful phonetics in the Chinese script: Their identification and characterization*. Doctoral dissertation. Rutgers University.

Kraemer, Stephen M. (1991a). *Sound clues in Mandarin character phonetic series*. Retrieved from https://scholarsbank.uoregon.edu/xmlui/handle/1794/4943

Kraemer, Stephen M. (1991b). *Levels of phonological regularity in the Chinese writing system.* Retrieved from https://scholarsbank.uoregon.edu/xmlui/handle/1794/8133

Kraemer, Stephen M. (2017a). *Let's Learn Mandarin Phonics. Seven Basic Phonetic Patterns of Commonly Occurring Chinese Characters.* CreateSpace Independent Publishing Platform.

Kraemer, Stephen M. (2017b). *Let's Learn Mandarin Phonics-2. Final and Final-Tone Perfect Phonetic Patterns of Common Chinese Characters.* CreateSpace Independent Publishing Platform.

Kraemer, Stephen M. (2018a). *Let's Learn Mandarin Phonics-3. Rime Clue, Rime-Tone Clue, Ending Clue, Ending-Tone Clue Phonetic Patterns of Common Chinese Characters.* CreateSpace Independent Publishing Platform.

Kraemer, Stephen M. (2018b). *Let's Learn Mandarin Phonics-4. Initial Clue, Initial-Tone Clue, Tone-Clue and Related Phonetic Patterns of Common Chinese Characters.* CreateSpace Independent Publishing Platform.

Kraemer, Stephen M. (2018c). *Let's Learn Mandarin Phonics-5. Vowel Phonetic Clues for Common Chinese Characters.* CreateSpace Independent Publishing Platform.

Kraemer, Stephen M. (2018d). *Phonetic Clues for Learning Common Chinese Characters.* CreateSpace Independent Publishing Platform.

Kraemer, Stephen M. (2018e). *A Phonetic Guide to Learning Chinese Characters.* CreateSpace Independent Publishing Platform.

Kraemer, Stephen M. (2018f). *Let's Learn Pinyin Final "i" Chinese Characters in Mandarin.* CreateSpace Independent Publishing Platform.

Kraemer, Stephen M. (2018g). *Homorganic Initial Patterns in Common Mandarin Chinese Characters*. CreateSpace Independent Publishing Platform.

Kraemer, Stephen M. (2018h). *Let's Learn Pinyin Final "u/ü" Patterns in Mandarin Chinese Characters*. CreateSpace Independent Publishing Platform.

Kraemer, Stephen M. (2018i). *Coronal Initial Patterns in Common Mandarin Chinese Characters.* CreateSpace Independent Publishing Platform.

Kraemer, Stephen M. (2018j). *Voiceless Alveolar/Retroflex Initial Patterns in Mandarin Chinese Characters.* CreateSpace Independent Publishing Platform.

Kraemer, Stephen M. (2018k). *Velar/Palatal Initial Patterns in Mandarin Chinese Characters.* CreateSpace Independent Publishing Platform.

Kraemer, Stephen M. (2018l). *Pinyin 'an' Rime Patterns in Mandarin Chinese Characters.* CreateSpace Independent Publishing Platform.

Kraemer, Stephen M. (2018m). *Let's Learn Pinyin "n/ng" Ending Patterns in Mandarin Chinese Characters.* CreateSpace Independent Publishing Platform.

Kraemer, Stephen M. (2018n). *Final Patterns in Pinyin "ng" Ending Mandarin Chinese Characters*. CreateSpace Independent Publishing Platform.

Kraemer, Stephen M. (2019). *Initial Perfect and Initial-Tone Perfect Patterns in Mandarin Chinese Characters*. Independent Publishing Platform.

Kraemer, Stephen M. (2019a). *Initial-Rime Perfect and Initial-Ending Perfect Patterns in Mandarin Chinese Characters.* Independent Publishing Platform.

Kraemer, Stephen M. (2019b). *Similar Vowel Patterns in Initial-Perfect Mandarin Chinese Characters.* Independent Publishing Platform.

Kraemer, Stephen M. (2019c). *Homorganic Variation in the Pronunciation of Chinese Characters in Mandarin.* Independent Publishing Platform.

Kratochvil, Paul. (1968). *The Chinese language today: Features of an emerging standard.* London: Hutchinson & Co., Ltd.

Xinhua zidian (New China dictionary). (1971). Beijing: Shangwu Yinshuguan.
[<新华字典>, 1971, 北京: 商务印书馆

Zhou, Youguang. (1980). *Hanzi shengpang duyin biancha* (A handy look up for the pronunciation of phonetics in Chinese characters). Jilin: Jilin Remnin Chubanshe.
[周 有光, 1980, <汉字声旁读音便查>, 吉林: 吉林人民出版社.]